Maths QED CLUB

Subtracting

Ann Montague-Smith

6−0=6

6−1=5

9−0=9

9−1=8

QED Publishing

QED

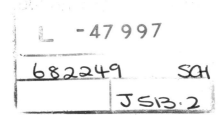
First published in the UK in 2005 by
QED Publishing
A Quarto Group company
226 City Road
London EC1V 2TT

www.qed-publishing.co.uk

A Catalogue record for this book is available from the British Library.

ISBN 1 84538 177 7

Written by Ann Montague-Smith
Designed and edited by The Complete Works
Illustrated by Peter Lawson
Photography by Steve Lumb

Publisher Steve Evans
Creative Director Louise Morley
Editorial Manager Jean Coppendale

Printed and bound in China

With thanks to:

Contents

Subtraction to 5   4

Finding differences   6

Taking away   8

Subtraction words   10

How many more?   12

Subtraction patterns   14

Taking away 9 or 11   16

Teen numbers   18

A subtraction problem   20

Supporting notes   22

Using this book   24

Subtraction to 5

Each toy box shows you how many toys go inside.
Count how many toys are outside the box.
How many toys are inside the box?

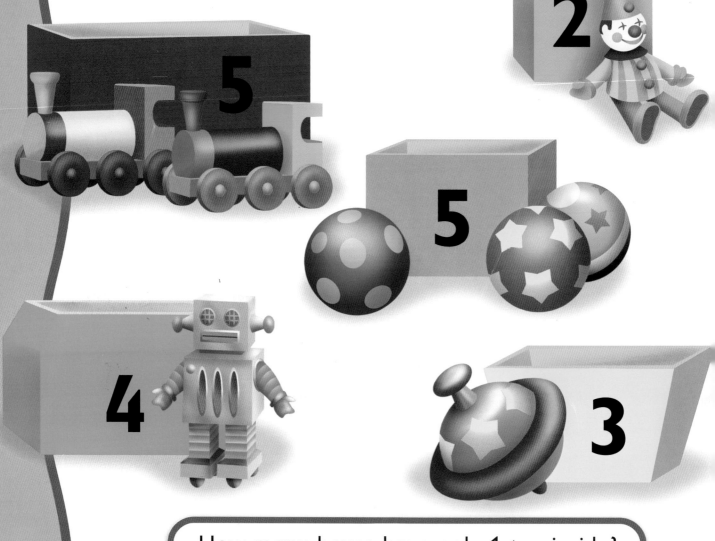

How many boxes have only 1 toy inside?

4

3

Try this

Do this with a friend.
You will need 8 counters and a cup.
Take turns to hide some of
the counters under a cup.
Ask your friend to count what is left.
Say, "How many counters
have I hidden?"

5

4

5

Finding differences

The numbers on the bags tell you how many gold pieces should be inside the bags. Say how many. Now count how many gold pieces each pirate has in his hand. So, how many gold pieces are in the bags?

Count up in ones from the lower number to the higher number to find the difference.

Challenge

Do this with a friend.

Take turns to say a number less than 9.
The other one works out the difference
between that number and 9.
Try this again for the difference
between a number and 11.

7

The difference between 7 and 9 is 2.

Taking away

Each monkey has some bananas. If you take away 3 bananas, how many will each of them have left?

Try this again. This time, take away 4 bananas.

Try this

Take away 5 from 6, 7, 8, 9, 10, 11 and 12. Write a subtraction sentence for each number. Tell someone the patterns that you can see.

6−5=1

Subtraction words

Play this game with a friend. You will need a 1–6 dice and 2 counters. Take turns to throw the dice. Move your counter along the path for the number shown on the dice. Answer the question on the path. If you get the question wrong, move back to where you were before. The first one to reach the *Finish* is the winner.

Start

$6-3=$

$5-1=$

What is 3 less than 7?

How much is 2 less than 8?

What is the difference between 10 and 1?

$12-8=$

$10-5=$

Take 6 from 7.

What is 7 minus 4?

$9-1=$

$10-0$

With a friend

Take turns to say any number between 0 and 10. The other one says the number that is left when your number is subtracted from 10. See how quickly you can play this game.

Say 2 numbers with a difference of 5.

9 subtract 2

What is 5 taken from 12?

How much more is 11 than 7?

How much more is 3 than 3?

10 subtract 8

Say two numbers with a difference of 3.

What is 10 take away 10?

Finish

How many less than 7 is 5?

9−7=

8−5=

How many more?

Look at one of the boys below. How many toys does he have? How many more toys does he need to make the number on his t-shirt?

Now work out how many more toys the other children need to make the number on their t-shirts.

10

Challenge

Try this with a friend.
Each of you draw a set of
toys with fewer than 7 in it.
Now swap drawings. Work out how
many more toys are needed to make
a set of 15. Try this 3 more times.

9

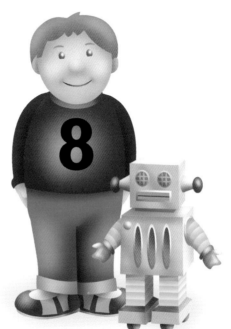

8

12

13

Subtraction patterns

Look at the subtraction sentences
that Lenny lion has written.
Work out what comes next in the
pattern. What would come after that?

5−0=5
5−1=4
5−2=3

10−0=10
10−1=9

7−0=7
7−1=6

4−0=4
4−1=3

8−0=8
8−1=7

Now try the other patterns.

14

6−0=6
6−1=5

Look at this number pattern
12−0=12   12−1=11.
Write the pattern so that you finish it.
Explain to an adult what patterns
you can see.

12−0=12

9−0=9
9−1=8

5−0=5
5−1=4

3−0=3
3−1=2

Taking away 9 or 11

There is a trick you can use when taking away 9. Take 16–9. Think of 16–10. Now add 1. Look at the sheep. If 9 run away, how many will be left? Take 9 away from the other sets of animals.

Now suppose 11 animals run away. Try –10 then –1. How many animals will be left in each set now?

Now try this

Eight animals have run away from each field. Think about how you could work this out by taking away 10. What would you need to add? How many animals are left in each field now?

Teen numbers

Look at the numbers on each flower. Find the difference between each pair. Remember: if you know that 9−5=4, then you can work out that 19−5=14.

Add 1 to the larger number. What is the difference now?

Now try this

Count on in ones from the smaller to the larger number. What is 22–17? What is 22–18? What is 22–19? What about 22–15 and 22–16?

18, 19, 20, 21, 22

19

A subtraction problem

Look at the numbers on the runners.
Find pairs of numbers which have
a difference of 3.

10

5

2

1

12

9

4

6

You may find it helpful to write some subtraction
sentences to remind you of the numbers you have tried.

Challenge

Write 10 pairs of numbers which have a difference of 4. Here is a subtraction sentence to start you off.

10−6=4

11

8

Finish

3

7

Supporting notes

Subtraction to 5 – pages 4-5

If the children do not yet know these subtraction facts, they will find it helpful to count on their fingers to find the answers, then to count along a number line. Encourage them next to count along a mental number line 'in their heads'.

Finding differences – pages 6-7

Begin by counting up from the lower to the higher number, keeping a track of how many on fingers. For example, for the difference between 4 and 7 count: 5, 6, 7. This gives a count of 3, which is the difference. With practise, the children will begin to make the count mentally.

Taking away – pages 8-9

Encourage the children to explain which strategy they used to take away. Some may still count on their fingers. If so, provide a 0 to 10 number line and use this to count on from the lower to the higher number. The children can keep a tally with their fingers. Progress to using a mental number line for counting on, where the children do not have recall of the answer.

Subtraction words – pages 10-11

This activity gives children practise in using subtraction vocabulary. Read the questions together. If the children do not have rapid recall of the answer, discuss how the answer could be found, such as counting up from the lower to the higher number, at first on fingers and then, when confident, along a mental number line.

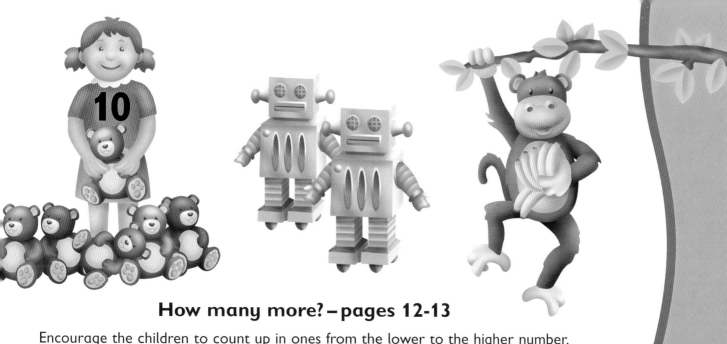

How many more? – pages 12-13

Encourage the children to count up in ones from the lower to the higher number. Encourage them to do this mentally. At first, they may need to keep track of the count by using their fingers. For the numbers 3 and 8 say, '4, 5, 6, 7, 8. So that is 5 that we counted. So we need 5 more than 3 to make 8.'

Subtraction patterns – pages 14-15

If children know a subtraction fact, then they can work out a closely related fact. For example, if they know 8−1=7, then they can work out that 8−2 is 6, or 1 less than before because 2 is 1 more than 1. Encourage them to use this as a mental strategy. They will find it useful at first to write out the sequence of subtraction sentences.

Taking away 9 or 11 – pages 16-17

The children will need to understand that if 10 is subtracted from any number, then it leaves the units unchanged. For example, 16−10 is 6. If children are unsure, at first use a number line so that they can count back 10, then add/subtract 1 to complete the calculation.

Teen numbers – pages 18-19

Encourage the children to use what they already know, or can calculate mentally, in order to work out what they do not know. If children are unclear about moving from, for example, 8−5=3 to 18−15=3, then use a number line and show them how this is the same as (10+8) − (10+5) or (10−10) + (8−5).

A subtraction problem – pages 20-21

Encourage the children to talk about which strategy they used to find the pairs with a difference of 3. Some may count on 3 from any of the numbers and look to see if the number they reach is there. Suggest that they begin with the smallest number, then the next smallest, and so on, so they work systematically.

Using this book

The illustrations in this book are bright, cheerful and colourful, and are designed to capture children's interest. Sit somewhere comfortable together, as you look at the book. Children of this age will usually need to have the instructional words on the pages read to them. Please read these to them, then encourage them to take part in the activity.

In this book, children are encouraged to work both practically, by counting pictures on the page, and mentally, by counting on or back 'in their heads'. When counting on, or back, children will find it useful to keep a tally of how many they have counted using their fingers. When they are confident with this, encourage them to do this mentally, without finger counting.

Subtracting covers a number of concepts. *Take away*, such as 'I have 5 apples. I give you 3. Now I have 2 left.' *Difference*, such as 'You have 5 oranges and I have 3. The difference between our oranges is 2.' This can also be seen as ideas of *more, less and fewer*, 'Who has more oranges? You or me? How many more? Who has fewer? You or me? How many fewer?' Children need to practise using the vocabulary of subtraction, such as take away, difference, minus, subtract, more, less, fewer, in practical activities, so that they experience using the vocabulary in realistic situations. As you work together through the pages of this book, do take time to ask the children to give answers as subtraction sentences. If you model using specific subtraction vocabulary, then they will learn how to use it.

Some of the activities in this book are games for two or more to play together. Play the game and make some 'deliberate' mistakes. This will challenge the children to spot the mistake and to correct you. This will help you to assess how well they understand and can use the mathematical idea which the pages are teaching.

Remember, learning about mathematics should always be a positive experience. So, enjoy together the mathematical games, activities and challenges in this book!